READING

BODY

LANGUAGE

By

Jordan D. Hunter

Human & Mind Center

TABLE OF CONTENT

INTRODUCTION 10

ORIGIN AND APPLICATION OF THIS DISCIPLINE 15
WHAT IS BODY LANGUAGE? 15
MOST PEOPLE GENERALLY DISPLAY A FEW CATEGORIES OF BODY
LANGUAGE 19
THE POWER OF BODY LANGUAGE 21
CHARACTERISTICS OF BODY LANGUAGE 23

HOW THE SUBCONSCIOUS LIMBIC SYSTEM DRIVES ALL BODY
LANGUAGE 26

MOST COMMON "SPOKEN BODY PARTS": FACE, THUMBS, FEET
AND EYELIDS: WHAT THEY SAID...31

THE NON-VERBAL COMMUNICATION AND SUBLIMINAL
MANIPULATION 48
WHAT IS NON-VERBAL COMMUNICATION? 48
KINDS OF NON-VERBAL COMMUNICATION.......................................50
ASSESSING NON-VERBAL SIGNALS 53
MIRRORING - MATCHING BODY LANGUAGE SIGNALS.......................63

EXAMPLES AND APPLICATIONS IN REAL LIFE 67
HOW TO USE BODY LANGUAGE IN PUBLIC SPEAKING 67

BODY LANGUAGE AT A BUSINESS MEETING OR MAKING A
PRESENTATION 79

SIX BODY LANGUAGE MISTAKES 87

How to Have a Positive Effect on Others 94

What can Mastering Body Language do for you? 97

More Postures for Improving your Levels of Performance .. 100

BODY LANGUAGE APPLICATIONS 108

The biological feedback mechanism of body language 116

Training and exercises 117

CONCLUSION 120

INTRODUCTION

Wouldn't it be nice to be able to read people like books? With just a look you could know whether this person is someone is being deceitful to you or not. You could get ahead of them and everything would be fine. This sounds too good to be true, right?

While it is not possible to read minds, you can get pretty close to clairvoyance with the tips in here. This is your guide to the fundamentals of reading people like books. You will learn everything you need to know about body language, facial expressions, nuances of speech, and other signs that reveal what a person is trying to conceal.

It may seem very difficult to figure out what a person is trying to hide. People may seem like obscure, impenetrable mysteries. But that is just because you don't know the cues and signs to watch for. Once you learn them, reading people is actually very easy. Some people make a living out of reading others. FBI profilers, cops, job interviewers, and even dating profile matchmakers are excellent reads of character who are adroit at finding out who people really are without being told. These people are not in possession of some secret superhuman talent. Rather, they have mastered tips and tricks that you can master yourself. This will help you become as good as an FBI profiler at reading other people.

You first have to learn some of the main tells that people exhibit. These tells not only betray when someone is lying, but they also indicate what a person is not saying. Tells give away what a person is hiding inside, whether or not the person is being dishonest. One of the best tells is any inconsistency between someone's talk and body language. Eye contact is another great tell. Fidgeting can indicate nervousness.

You can glean a lot of information about people by what they do directly say, however. People are surprisingly open. You just have to pay attention. Learning to read people involves learning to really listen and absorb what someone says to you.

Furthermore, you must learn to make people want to open up to you. You can make yourself the type of person that people want to talk to. You want to project an aura of caring and compassion that make others trust you and feel comfortable around you. There are so many different ways to read people. From being introspective to carefully observing others.

You may wonder why reading people is so important. There are countless benefits to being able to understand the people around you right off the bat. Your understanding of people can certainly make your life easier.

For one thing, you can become a more sensitive and empathetic lover and friend because you understand people better. You can read the signs of someone's emotions and respond appropriately. You will no longer be clueless about what those around you feel.

You also can avoid a lot of pain and problems by learning to identify the true intentions of people.

Some people are just bad. Most bad people are good at hiding it, however. You can see through their ruses and protect yourself. On the flip side, you can spot good people who will treat you well. As a result, you can avoid bad friends and pick good ones. Your dating life will improve as well as you become more discerning about your partners.

Work can become easier. If you work in sales or customer service, you will be able to read your customers for clues about whether or not they are happy. If you work for clients, you can understand their wants better. You can become more empathetic and understanding of co-workers and superiors. This can help you satisfy people that you work with better.

In addition, you will get along better with your family. By being able to read your family members, you can tell what they are feeling and what they expect. Fights over "nothing" will stop because you will be able to spot the warning signs that a fight is coming. You will also be more empathetic, which your family members will appreciate.

Even on the street, you can become more discerning about the intentions of others. You can spot people who mean you harm and take steps to protect yourself. This is quite important for self-defense.

The life skill of people reading is very helpful and essential to your success in your social life. Therefore, you should start learning today.

ORIGIN AND APPLICATION OF THIS DISCIPLINE

WHAT IS BODY LANGUAGE?

We sometimes do things without knowing that we do them, much like a nervous habit, such as tapping your foot or rubbing your hands together. Though we may not be aware that we are doing these things, others see these habits and read into them. We may be seen as nervous or agitated by others due to these unconscious behaviors that we are prone to.

At other times, we might engage in an action or pose with a certain intent that is consciously chosen. We can choose to turn our bodies towards someone we are busy talking to to seem more attentive. Imagine your first job interview: you cautiously keep yourself from twitching, rubbing your face, or slouching. You have been made aware by various knowledgeable people such as school counselors and career guides to be aware of these interview bombs. Knowing how bad these make you seem; you learn not to engage in this form of body language.

We can lie with a written and spoken language. Usually, we lie to avoid getting into trouble. Likewise, we can also lie with our bodies. We can project a body image that is disingenuous and has been carefully polished to accomplish a certain appearance. I imagine that several of us have been caught in a scam at some point in time, and this is an ideal example of how clever users of body language can manipulate it to convince us of their honesty. We get people to believe us, based on what we show, and not what we say.

In expressing emotions, facial expression is important. It combines the movement of the cheeks, nose, lips, eyebrows and eyes to show the various moods of a person. Some researchers showed that body and facial expressions complement each other in interpreting emotions. Some experiments recognized the influence of

16

body expression in recognizing facial expression, which means that the brain processes both body and facial expressions simultaneously.

Body postures can also detect emotions. For example, if an individual is angry, he will try to dominate another person. His posture will show such approach tendencies. If he is fearful, his approach will be that of avoidance. He will feel submissive and weak. Aside from body postures and facial expressions, gestures also have different interpretations.

For example, if a person folds his arms during a discussion, it may mean that he is not willing to listen to the speaker or he has a closed mind. If he crosses his arms over the other, it means he lacks confidence and is insecure.

Relaxed hand gestures show that the individual is self-assured and confident while clenched hands can mean that he is either angry or stressed. If he wrings his hands, it means he is anxious and nervous. Finger gestures show the overall well-being of an individual. In some cultures, it is acceptable to point with an index finger. Handshakes also show the levels of emotion and confidence of individuals. They are popular in some cultures. In Muslim cultures, a man cannot shake or touch the hands of a woman. In Hindu cultures, a man greets a woman by keeping his hands together like when he is praying.

When it comes to learning how to read body language, the main goal is trying to determine if the person in front of you is being genuine. Body language clues are extremely crucial when trying to decipher someone's innermost thoughts, personality, and even intentions. In many ways, body language teaches you to become a human lie detector. Humans can be great liars, but while we may have been able to trick our mind into saying words we do not mean, we cannot trick our body into executing the lie perfectly.

Being able to read body language is an excellent skill to have in situations such as job interviews, when you are trying to solve a crime or resolve conflict.

Being able to see beneath the surface into what is going on inside someone's mind will help you make better, more informed decisions.

What makes body language so tricky a skill to master is the need to decipher body language cues within the right context. For example, when a person crosses his or her arms in front of the chest, you could construe that as negative body language, perhaps an indicator that the person is not happy to be here. However, depending on the context, it could also mean that the person is feeling cold, uncomfortable, or frustrated. Not accounting for the context of a situation can lead to misreading of body language cues and a wrong conclusion.

MOST PEOPLE GENERALLY DISPLAY A FEW CATEGORIES OF BODY LANGUAGE

Dominant: Dominant body language comes into play when someone wants to be in command. The most standout cue for this category of body language is someone standing tall, with his or her chest puffed out.

Attentive

This shows someone's interest and engagement with the conversation or situation.

Bored:

A common representation of this body language is the lack of eye contact and constant yawning.

Aggressive:

An aggressive person will display threatening body language cues.

Defensive:

A defensive person will look as if he or she is protecting or withholding information.

Closed Off:

You can recognize a closed off person by noticing if he or she is shutting you off by crossing his or her arms and guardedly standing farther away from you.

Open:

This body language is friendly and welcoming.

Emotional:

We normally display this body language when we feel heavily influenced current feelings and usually have changing moods.

THE POWER OF BODY LANGUAGE

Body language extends beyond more than just the four types mentioned. It can also be divided into positive and negative body language. Positive body language draws people towards you and creates a sense of belonging and accomplishment. This includes things such as encouraging smiles, firm handshakes, making eye contact, facing someone with your body in a neutral position, and using an encouraging tone of voice. Negative body language is based on avoidance. It includes turning your back on someone, not facing them when they speak, looking down, using a soft and insecure tone of voice, and avoiding eye contact. When someone uses these body languages tells, we begin to assume the worst about that person. We see them as being dishonest, uninvested, and disinterested.

Knowing these two forms of body language, which would you choose to look at? In all likelihood, you would prefer seeing the positive body language. We want to feel acknowledged and valued during our communications with other people. Seeing someone face you, look you in the eye, speak in a clear tone without hiding their mouth, and have an honest appearance due to their open posture is very encouraging and ensures that communication can happen harmoniously and smoothly.

Yet, we often use the negative body language ourselves when we feel intimidated or unsure of a situation. Being skilled at using your body language would help you to achieve more favorable outcomes from your daily interactions and communications.

The power of body language according to Guilbeault (2018) lies in that it can help you gain things that you want, such as friends or jobs; however, it can also make you lose the things you want because of using the negative body language forms. It can cost you your job, friends, and even intimate relationships. Without even opening our mouths, we can attract or repel people. Body language can build trust, and this is the key ingredient in all relationships, whether for work, for companionship, or for intimacy. Using the power of body language, you can lead a more productive and successful life. Hence, it is well worth learning the skills of recognizing body language and its meaning in others and ourselves.

CHARACTERISTICS OF BODY LANGUAGE

In general, body language is the manifestation of the emotions of an individual, meaning it can be perceived by another person. First, it is understood that the signal from the body language to the receiver can be highly complicated.

An individual's body language consists of multiple body parts moving or not moving together, and all must be taken into account to interpret the emotion of a specific person. A specific facial expression taken out of context from the person's other bodily reactions will give an incomplete or otherwise misleading analysis of his or her emotions. Another characteristic is that the projected emotion from body language is perceived automatically in a way similar to speech. This characteristic makes nonverbal interaction spontaneous, as there is often little need to further interpret what an individual means with his or her body language.

A third characteristic is that young individuals can acquire and develop body language very easily and rapidly. Children learn what gestures and facial expressions mean from their parents, friends and even strangers who interact with them. The ease of acquiring knowledge of body language can make children carry on specific body languages into their maturity.

How the Subconscious Limbic System Drives All Body Language

The reason nonverbal language never lies is that it happens unconsciously. We have the ability to consciously control the things we say in order to lie or share half-truths, but the body will still show the truth, why does this happen?

Humans have evolved to communicate in a nonverbal manner. There is an ancient system that lives inside our brain that understands and conveys intentions or emotions through physical movements. This part of the brain is what is called the limbic system. It works in a precise manner. The amygdala is the key player in the limbic system and is located in the medial temporal lobe. It works by helping us to process emotions.

There is an interesting evolutionary story that explains how the limbic system cam to be. It takes us through how water-dwelling creatures became land roaming and continues to turn into walking, talking, and hunting humans.

Something that is hard to believe for most is that creatures have evolved from common ancestors. These ancestors lived in the water 360 million years ago. The struggle to survive and climatic changes forced them to move to the land. Their fins turned into limbs in order to walk, and their skin became tougher in order to handle the harsh climate.

About 320 to 310 million years ago, the reptile evolved. This was when the limbic system began to develop. The reflexive system of the breed, feed, flight, and the fight began. The part of the brain this created consisted of the cerebellum and brain stem. The behavior of the reptile is predictable, but it is what helped them to survive. Emotions didn't exist until mammals evolved.

When mammals emerged, they had a deliberate social behavior, unlike their reptile ancestors. The reason for this could be connected to their habitation, bonding, nurturing, reproduction, and changed metabolism. A mammal's offspring grows inside of them until they reach a certain stage. They are feed by secretions from the mammary glands, and they control their temperature in order to adjust to different climates.

The new brain structure, called the cortex, for mammals was built upon the reptilian complex. Even though mammals were superior in their survival, they naturally used the fight or flight approach, which is a reptilian act. They created other ways to work around this fight or flight approach through planned movements, expressions, and behavior. Emotions were a great gift as well as being able to smell different things and being able to remember them. This helped mammals to endure different circumstances. This caused them to spread across the planet.

Finally, the common ancestors of apes and humans appeared the primate. It is possible that they evolved from mammals that were more skilled at climbing trees for shelter and food. The primate's brain developed more complex parts to help them adapt to new environments and social challenges. They have better systems to coordinate movements on the ground and in trees. They had the ability to plan and think. Their vision also improved, and they could recall scenes.

As the climate changed, parts of these primates remained in wooded areas, leaving in the trees. Others were forced to start roaming the ground when their trees were replaced by brush. These primates start to walk on two legs with the hands-free to farm, fish, hunt, make tools and gather food. They start to build and live-in fixed shelters.

This ability to walk on two feet changed their movement and behavior patterns and how they communicated. Making different sounds, gestures, and facial expressions became helpful in express their feelings to the other people in their group. Through various civilizations, this continues to be a diverse part of their lifestyle and communication. This created their cultural and social norms and ethics. For us, modern humans, the neocortex is the most advanced part of the brain. This is also the area that helps us to regulate our emotions, harbor feelings, and control a few of the impulses of our limbic system. The limbic brain is what controls all of our nonverbal communication, and we can't completely control it with our neocortex.

Emotional and visual memory has the ability to cause us to act in ways that our ancestors would. We feel comfortable in favorable situations and uncomfortable when in danger or distress. When we are placed in a threatening situation, we are still going to act like other mammals or reptiles.

Most Common "Spoken Body Parts": Face, Thumbs, Feet and Eyelids: What They Said

Posture

There's a good reason our parents always told us to stand or sit up straight. A sloucher looks weak and submissive, while the person with good posture looks confident and assertive. This is well within reason. When we slouch, we restrict the flow of oxygen to our lungs, and we make ourselves appear smaller. This kind of posture puts unnecessary strain on our neck and back muscles.

Overall, it strains our body, reduces the flow of energy in our body and makes us look unattractive. What do we do when we are exhausted and ready to give up? We slouch. To overcome slouching, one needs to strengthen the back and torso by exercising (yoga is helpful) as well as by staying mindful of and practicing good posture until it becomes a habit.

A healthy diet will also help strengthen your bones and muscles as well as give you a more positive outlook on life. If it does not come naturally to you, you'll have to make an extra effort to improve your posture. It may be a little difficult, but it's not impossible, and it will be worth the effort.

The eyes

The cliché that the eyes are the mirrors to the soul may have some truth in it. When a person is positively stimulated by what he sees, his eyes open wider, his pupils dilate, and his eyebrows are raised.

Eyebrows that are raised make a face mimic that of a baby's and arouse protective emotions from others, especially from males toward females. This is the reason plucked eyebrows on women make them more attractive to the opposite sex. On the other hand, lowered brows show authority and seriousness.

Arms

The chest contains the heart and lungs, vital organs in the human body. It is no wonder that, when we feel threatened, we automatically cross our arms over our chest to protect ourselves. Folding the arms over the chest is a way of making a barrier between our vital organs and whatever it is that we find threatening. This is a sign that a person feels negative about what he hears, or that he feels defensive or uneasy. Sometimes, the individual tries to relax his arms, but his legs remain crossed.

Conversely, studies have shown that folding one's arms during a lecture can impede learning and retention of information. Intentional folding of the arms seems to signal to our brains to be cautious and skeptical about what we hear. At the same time, we send out signals to others that we are not being friendly or accommodating.

The arms are a sort of barrier for protecting vulnerable parts of the body. Men are observed to unconsciously cover their private parts when feeling insecure or dejected. Sometimes, people cross their arms and clutch at themselves to give a self-reassuring "self-hug."

The thumbs

The thumbs symbolize authority, superiority and power. A showing of thumbs is a showing of confidence or a feeling of superiority. A person may tuck his hands in his front pockets with his thumbs out of the pockets. He is showing that he feels in power or superior.

If he keeps his hands in his back pockets, but still with his thumbs out; he is trying to conceal his feelings of superiority. When a person points to another using his thumb, it might signal that he's about to criticize that person or that he looks down on that person. We know that crossing or folding one's arms over the chest shows resistance or disagreement. If a person has his arms crossed with his thumbs up, he is resistant and at the same time feels superior to the speaker.

The legs

We've gone through the face or head, eyes and hands. Experts have determined that the further the part of the body is from the brain, the less we can fake its movements. Needless to say, some people may have mastered the art of faking their face and hand movements but have absolutely no control of their leg movements. Many of us are hardly even aware of what our legs are doing while we're talking.

Originally, our legs were meant to take us to our destination and to take us away from any perceived danger. To this day, and if one observes carefully, the legs always point to where the owner wants to go.

The Head

Head movements can be quite easy to read if you know how to. Unfortunately, not everyone knows how to do this, which is why even the most obvious head movements go unnoticed by the ignorant and inexperienced person.

Let us take a look at the most common head movements alongside what they may be possibly indicating.

Let's start with a nod. In most parts of the world, a nod indicates encouragement. However, not all nods are made equally. When a person nods slowly, especially if they are doing it unconsciously, it connotes a deep level of interest or rapt attention. Another head movement that indicates interest is when the person tilts their head sideways. if you are making some form of presentation in class or at a meeting and you notice these two head movements, it is very likely that your points are well expressed and understood.

Hurried nods or frequent nods during a presentation could signal disinterest like in the second example above. If you notice this during your presentation or discussion, change your tactics or presentation style. Alternatively, pause the presentation and ask for input from the other person or people.

In the case where a person tilts their head back while you are talking with them, it is a possible sign of disbelief, doubt, or suspicion. Whether it is a one-on-one conversation or a formal presentation in front of a board of directors, take a moment to clarify what you were talking about before you noticed that head movement. If you are unsure, ask them if there is something, they would like you to make clearer. You could say, "I'm getting the feeling that you may need some further clarifications. Would you like me to clarify my last point or something I've said?"

When talking with a friend and they begin to scratch an imaginary itch on their necks or the side of their face or their jaw, this is usually body language of disagreement. Give the other person room to speak their mind by saying something along the lines of, "It looks like you have something different in mind. What is it?" This can also happen when you are speaking in a formal meeting. In the event that you are leading the discussions or in the case where it is appropriate for that particular meeting, you can give the person with the disagreeing body language a chance to say what's on their mind. You could say, "I see Mr. X has something to say. Would you please give us your point of view on this?"

In an official meeting, head movements can tell you who is in charge or who wields more authority. In a meeting, most heads will be turned towards the person who has the most authority.

The use of head movement is not limited to only formal meetings and during chitchats with friends. It can also speak volumes even in situations that do not require discussions. When someone stands with their head held upwards, it can signify arrogance, self-confidence, or superiority. This is especially true if their chin points forward.

Head held downwards could indicate a negative attitude or aggression. Subconsciously, our minds know that our intentions are not pure. Therefore, it makes us unconsciously protect our neck and throat, which are vulnerable parts of our body, by lowering our heads to cover them. This is subconscious body language to keep us safe in case the other person attacks us if they get wind of our intentions.

The last head movement I shall discuss is the head bobble. This is usually seen in places like India. It does not indicate a no or a yes. Instead, it can indicate a greeting, "yes," "no," "thank you," and even "maybe" depending on the circumstances in which it is used coupled with very slight alterations that are completely lost on a foreigner. Here's the point of all this: if you happen to visit any foreign country, you can build rapport with the natives by copying their customs and culture. Even if you do not get it perfectly, they will be glad that you respect them and want to learn about them.

The Face

The face conveys messages that are very obvious to notice. Expressions such as frowns, smiles (grin or smirk), grimaces, dropped jaw, squinting, raised eyebrows, yawns and so on can be read by almost everyone. Since it is not difficult to decode the emotional intent (anger, excitement, surprise, fear, confusion, disgust, and so on) by simply looking at the face, most of us have learned how to effectively hide these indicators so that we can appear polite. The following are some of the facial expressions and what they signify.

A smile is one body language cue that has a universal meaning. Even infants can read this nonverbal cue. It strongly indicates acceptance, agreement, and comfortableness. When a smile spreads to cover the entire face, it is genuine.

When a smile doesn't reach the eyes of the giver – when there are no crinkles at the corners of their eyes – it shows that it is a forced or fake smile. There are several reasons a person would want to wear a fake smile. They may want to be polite; they may want to be deceitful, or they simply want to seek approval from another person, especially from someone superior.

A slight smile accompanied by a slightly raised eyebrow is one facial expression that indicates confidence and friendliness. When you are talking with someone and notice this expression on the person's face, it indicates that they believe what you are saying.

If you are the one wearing this expression, you are conveying to the other person that you are trustworthy.

The lips are used for smiling and also for telling truth or falsehood. When someone touches their lips repeatedly while telling you something supposedly confidential, there is a high chance that they are withholding some of the information from you.

The Shoulders

Shrugging is usually considered as a sign of ignorance or cluelessness. However, it can indicate other things such as an unconscious need to protect our necks (vulnerable part) from danger. For example, notice how people generally react with they hear a sudden loud bang of a gun or even a seemingly harmless things like a balloon bursting. The first reaction for most people is to raise their shoulders to hide their neck. You can also observe this when people walk in front of a crowd that is focused on something, like a movie in a cinema. The person walking in front of the crowd tends to shrug so that their necks are hidden inside their shoulders in an unconscious attempt to protect themselves in case of an attack from the angry crowd. Even children speak this unconscious protective body language when they hide their necks by raising their shoulders if their parents attempt to hit them.

Hand Movements and Gestures

Keep your hands out of your pocket if you want to communicate openness and honesty. When you have your hands in your pocket, your body language is saying you don't have self-confidence, you are hiding something, or you are being defensive. When someone has their palms facing up as they are talking, that gesture strongly suggests that they are being honest. It does not necessarily mean that their views are correct, but it does show that they are genuinely expressing their thoughts.

Someone holding an object between you and them is unconsciously trying to put a barrier between you and them. Their body language is indicating that they are looking for any excuse to block you out.

When someone habitually points to another person while talking in a group or in a meeting, it is a strong indication that they have many things in common or they have some type of affinity. Here's a great way you can use that to your advantage, especially in a situation where you are canvassing for support: seek the support of one of the pairs, and you are most likely to get the support of the other.

Feet, Legs, Posture – ATTENTION!

When a physical appearance manifests itself in one's posture, you know the person is generally experiencing a strong feeling. If someone has started stomping the ground like a maniac, you can perceive that as someone attempting to scare you or someone releasing built up tension or anger. Closely related to the sad slouch though, is the happy and relaxed slouch. It's easy to spot the difference from the general energy of the person. If the shoulders are pushed back and the face is open, then it is a sign someone is happy. If you are struggling to see their face, then it is likely they are sad. If you are feeling sad you can go some way to reversing it by intentionally breathing deeply and gently and trying to dissolve your negativity by focusing it 'out' of yourself by adopting a posture that opens your chest up to the world and makes you stand taller.

Whether a person is simply standing or sitting can convey a lot. Standing suggests a person is active and ready to start thinking or moving, you rarely begin something energetic by first sitting down. This is useful to remember if you are meeting someone and trying to make a good impression, if you are standing you are open to playing around with personal space and touching, and it allows for greater use of powerful body language that isn't available if you are sitting down. Walking is a great way of using the vibrancy of standing and induces quick thinking in some and also puts the other person at ease by avoiding excessive eye contact. It is also an excellent way of mirroring another person, building rapport, and sharing energy because you have to commit to a similar pace to walk with another person.

Sitting is still a standard requirement in life though, so you need to be aware of what that portrays. It's easy to become too relaxed when sitting, which could demonstrate to others that you are tired or unenthusiastic, you might naturally do this by flopping your limbs around and tilting your head back.

Head

The head is one of the most important features because it's one of the main focuses of attention when we look at another person. The way we instantly make eye contact with people is quite phenomenal. A little experiment you can personally do is to look at a light for a brief period so that you have the imprint of the light in your vision while you are in a crowded area. Obviously be careful not to stare too long, but what you will find by paying attention to that light imprint is that when looking at people in the crowd you will be drawn like a magnet to their eyes.

The head itself is an important place for making gestures, next to your hands it's the second most common physical asset you have for indicating towards things. The state of your head's droopiness is an indication of many things: when sad or contemplative you will arch your neck down and stare at the ground, while feeling confident you will tend to look upwards and with sustained eye contact.

Head shaking is another way you can communicate strongly. Nodding up and down is obviously a way to reply to a question, but a slight

46

nod is a good way of telling someone you are paying attention. Often people that are meshing well, bob along together like toys on a car dashboard. A very fast paced nod might be an indication you want the speaker to hurry up or that you agree with what they are saying.

A quick whip or nod of the head is a good way of saying hello, it provides acknowledgement, and usually discourages engaging in a conversation. This can be useful if you've forgotten a name (you won't ever have to forget a name again once you've gotten your free bonus!) or you are in a hurry. If you lean into a nod it can have an almost "how do you do?" feel to it with a tip of the hat.

Boredom and interest are two types of gestures that can be easily read from the posture of the head. Propping your head up with your hands can say "I would rather be asleep" if the eyes are vacant or darting, or it can say "I am enraptured by your every word" if you are pushing the chin up for a better view.

THE NON-VERBAL COMMUNICATION AND SUBLIMINAL MANIPULATION

WHAT IS NON-VERBAL COMMUNICATION?

The non-verbal communication is the utilization of physical conduct, articulations, and traits to impart non-verbally, frequently accomplished more naturally, as opposed to deliberately.

Regardless of whether you are mindful of it or not, when you connect with others, you are ceaselessly giving and getting a silent sign. The majority of your non-verbal practices—the motions you make, your stance, your manner of speaking, the amount of eye-to-eye connection you make—all send strong messages.

They can ease individuals, build trust, and draw others toward you—or they can insult, confound, and undermine what you're attempting to impart.

These messages don't end when you cease talking, either. On certain occasions, what leaves your mouth and what you deliver through your non-verbal communication would possibly be two very different things.

When regarded with such a blended sign, the target audience wants to pick whether to receive your verbal or non-verbal message. Since the non-verbal exchange is a distinctive, spontaneous language that communicates your real feelings and expectations, they will more likely pick out that.

In any case, by enhancing how you comprehend and make use of non-verbal communication, you can categorize what you mean, associate higher with others, and build fulfilling connections with a much stronger foundation.

Kinds of Non-Verbal Communication

There are many different kinds of non-verbal communication or non-verbal exchange, including these:

Outward appearances

The human face is very expressive, equipped to express countless feelings without saying a word.

Body improvement and stance

Think about how your views of people are influenced by the manner in which they sit, walk, stand, or hold their head. Likewise, the manner in which you deliver and maintain yourself imparts an abundance of information to the world.

Motions

Signals are woven into our daily lives. You may also wave, point, call or make use of your hands when communicating in order to make your message even clearer, as opposed to when you only use verbal cues. However, some hand signals differ in meaning across different countries or cultures, so it is essential to be cautious about how you use motions in delivering your message without being misinterpreted by the receiver.

Eye-to-eye connection

Since the visual sense is overwhelming for the great majority, eye-to-eye connection are all a huge part of non-verbal communication. The manner in which you see somebody can convey numerous things, such as interest, love, threatening vibe, or fascination. Eye-to-eye connection is likewise important in maintaining the progression of the discussion and for checking the other individual's reaction to your message.

Contact

We bring a lot into the conversation through touch. Consider the special messages given by way of a handshake, a hug, or holding close someone, for instance.

Space

Have you ever felt awkward in the course of a conversation because the other person was standing too close, and you felt that your space was being invaded? We all have a need for personal space, regardless of the fact that this need varies depending on our culture, situation, and relationship with the other person.

Voice

It's not precisely what you state; it's the manner in which you say it. When you talk, different humans "read" your voice, nevertheless listening to your words. Things that they focus on include your pace, volume, tone, articulation, and mannerisms (e.g., saying "ahh" and "uh-huh"). Pay attention to how your way of speaking can exhibit mockery, anger, love, or uncertainty.

Assessing Non-Verbal Signals

Eye-to-eye connection

Is the person looking? Assuming this is the case, is it excessive or just normal?

Outward appearance

How does their face appear? Is it masklike and unexpressive, or is it truly present and loaded up with intrigue?

Manner of talking

Does the individual's voice project warmth, certainty, and intrigue—or is it careworn and blocked?

Posture and movement

Are their body unfastened or firm and fixed? Are their shoulders anxious and raised?

Contact

Is there any physical contact? Is it fitting to the circumstance? Does it make you feel awkward?

Force

Does the person show up to be level-headed, cool, and impartial—or are they over-the-top and exaggerated?

Timing and position

Are there an easy progression of timing forward and backward? Do non-verbal reactions come too unexpectedly or too gradually?

Sounds

Do you hear sounds that show enthusiasm, mindfulness, or fear from the individual?

Expressions

The six widespread outward appearances - perceived the world over It is presently commonly acknowledged that specific fundamental outward appearances of human feelings are perceived far and wide - and that the utilization and acknowledgment of these expressions are hereditarily acquired as opposed to socially molded or learned. While there have been seen as minor varieties and contrasts among indefinitely disengaged clans' individuals, the accompanying fundamental human feelings are commonly utilized, perceived, and part of mankind's hereditary character these enthusiastic face expressions are:

- Happiness
- Sadness
- Fear
- Disgust
- Surprise
- Anger

The utilization and acknowledgment of outward appearances to pass on certain essential human feelings is a piece of developed human nature, hereditarily acquired, and not subject to social learning or molding.

Proxemics

Proxemics is a fancy word used in the body language community to mean the study of personal space and proximity. You can't truly read someone's body language without noticing where they are in relation to you in space.

Someone seems to be paying attention to you, they have open body language, they are even pointing themselves towards you – so they're clearly paying attention to you right? Well, maybe not if they're on the other side of the room and not moving any closer towards you. When it comes to reading other people, certain elements of personal space are obvious. If someone is close it will mean they are, or are trying to be, more intimate. However, with some people, especially men, there is a tendency to be territorial and to feel they have more access to your personal space than you might feel comfortable with.

You can use these cues to determine if someone is being aggressive, friendly, or flirtatious. By reading the rest of someone's body language you can see if they are leaning towards you to be friendly or to be assertive. It is quite risky to try and invade other people's personal space to get an advantage over them so in general try to avoid getting too close to someone unless they invite you to by touching you or speaking at a lower volume that requires you to lean in.

Touch

We engage in touching routinely. We commonly shake hands as greetings or assign to signal shared understanding. Touch as a form of communication is called haptics. For children, touch is a crucial aspect of their development. Children that do not get adequate touch have developmental issues. Touch helps babies cope with stress. At infancy, touch is the first sense that infants respond to.

Functional Touch

At the workplace, touch is among effective means of communication, but it is necessary to keep it professional or casual. For instance, handshakes are often exchanged within a professional environment and can convey a trusting relationship between two people. Pay attention to the nonverbal cues that you are sending next time you shake someone's hand.

Overall, one should always convey confidence when shaking another person's hand, but you should avoid being overly confident. Praise and encouragement are communicated by a firm pat on the back. Remember, people have varied reactions to touch as nonverbal communication. For instance, an innocent touch can make another person feel uncomfortable or frightened.

Touch can become particularly complicated when touch is between a boss and a subordinate. Generally, those in power will utilize touch with subordinates to reinforce the hierarchy of the workplace. It is usually not acceptable for it to occur the other way around. For this reason, you should make sure to be careful even in the instance of using the most trivial of touches and resolve to enhance your communication techniques with your juniors.

A standard measure is that it is better to fail but remain on the side of caution. Functional touch includes being physically examined by a doctor and being touch as a form of professional massage.

Social Touch

In the United States, a handshake is the most common way one engages in social touching. Handshakes vary from culture to culture, though. In some countries, kissing one or both cheeks are more common than a handshake.

In the same interactions, men will allow a male stranger to touch them on their shoulders and arms whereas women feel comfortable being touched by a female stranger only on the arms.

Men are likely to enjoy touch from a female stranger while women tend to feel uncomfortable with any touch by a male stranger. Equally important, men and women process touch differently which can create confusing and awkward situations. One should be respectful and cautious.

For instance, while you stand close to a stranger on an elevator, it is not acceptable to stand so close to them that you make contact with him or her.

Friendship Touch

The types of touches allowed between friends vary depending on the context. For instance, women are more receptive touching female friends compared to their male counterparts. Touch is different depending on the closeness of the family and the sex of the family member.

Displays of affection between friends are almost always appreciated and necessary, even if you are not a touchy person. One should be willing to get out of their comfort zone and offer their friend a hug when he or she is struggling. Helping others enliven their moods is likely to uplift your moods as well.

Intimacy Touch

In romantic relationships, touches that communicate love play a critical role. For instance, the simplest of touches can convey a critical meaning such as holding hands or placing your arm around your partner which communicates that you are together.

Adults place more emphasis on nonverbal cues compared to verbal cues when communicating according to recent studies on communication. In the early stages of dating, men tend to initiate physical contact in line with societal norms, but in later stages, it is women that initiate contact. Women place more premiums on touch compared to men and even the smallest of gestures can help calm women they were upset.

Arousal Touch

Arousing touches are elicited by intense feelings and are only acceptable when mutually agreed upon. Arousal touches are meant to evoke pleasure and can involve kissing, hugging, and flirtatious touching, and are often intended to suggest sex. One should be careful about their partner's needs. One can greatly improve their communication skills and relationships by considering the nonverbal messages you send via touching behavior.

Additionally, our sense of touch is intended to communicate clearly and quickly. Touch can elicit subconscious communication. For instance, you instantly pull away from your hand when touching something hot even before you consciously process. In this manner, touch constitutes one of the quickest ways to communicate. Touch as a form of nonverbal communication is an instinctive form of communication.

In detail, touch conveys information instantly and causes a guttural reaction. Completely withholding touch will communicate the wrong messages without your realization.

MIRRORING - MATCHING BODY LANGUAGE SIGNALS

At the point when body language and discourse attributes are reflected or synchronized between individuals, this will, in general, help the way toward making and keeping affinity (a common sentiment of sympathy, getting, trust).

The term synchronized is apparently an increasingly exact specialized term on the grounds that mirroring suggests visual signals just when the standards of coordinating body language stretch out to discernible signals additionally - strikingly discourse pace, pitch, tone, and so on.

'Reflected' or synchronized body language between two individuals supports sentiments of trust and compatibility since it creates oblivious sentiments of confirmation.

At the point when someone else shows comparable body language to our own, this causes us to respond unknowingly to feel, "This individual resembles me and concurs with the manner in which I am. I like this individual since we are comparative, and he/she enjoys me as well."

The opposite impact applies. At the point when two individuals' body language signals are unique - i.e., not synchronized - they feel less like one another, and the commitment is less agreeable. Every individual detects a contention emerging from the crisscrossing of signals - the two individuals are not attesting one another; rather, the confused signals convert into oblivious sentiments of conflict, inconvenience, or even dismissal. The oblivious mind thinks, "This individual doesn't care for me; he/she is diverse to me. I am not being asserted. Consequently, I feel cautious."

Backers and clients of NLP (Neuro-Linguistic Programming) use mirroring deliberately, as a strategy for 'getting on top of' someone else, and with somewhat practice can initially match and afterward really and tenderly to change the signals - and as far as anyone knows in this manner the sentiments and mentalities - of others, utilizing mirroring systems.

Discourse pace or speed is a model. At the point when you are talking with somebody, first match their pace of talking, at that point tenderly change your pace - more slow or quicker - and check whether the other individual tails you. Frequently they will do.

Individuals, for the most part being quite helpful spirits, regularly normally coordinate one another. To do in any case can once in a while feel awkward, despite the fact that we once in a while ponder it.

At the point when someone else inclines forward towards us at a table, we regularly reflect and do similarly. At the point when they recline and unwind, we do likewise.

Sales reps and other expert communicators are generally educated to reflect a wide range of increasingly inconspicuous signals as a method for making trust and compatibility with the other individual and to impact frames of mind.

Mirroring right now isn't just replicating or impersonating. Mirroring is powerful when developments and gestures are reflected likewise, so the impact stays oblivious and inconspicuous. Clear replicating would be viewed as unusual or annoying.

Examples and Applications in Real Life

How to Use Body Language in Public Speaking

A type of nonverbal communication that is premised on the qualities of voice and the manner one vocalizes them is known as paralinguistic. The accent, pitch, and tone of our voice communicate more about us and our personality. Our accent can tell where we come from or our teachers. The audience will for instance form stereotypes based on your accent. An individual that talks slow may sound tired, thoughtful or perhaps not intelligent. An individual that talks fast may sound shady, anxious or excited. Inflection, vocal volume and stammering do influence verbal messages and affect the processing of the intended meaning by the audience. In this manner, paralinguistic entails the aspects of spoken communication that does not involve words. For this reason, paralinguistic emphasize or diminish the intended meaning of what people say. Other aspects of body language are part of paralinguistic. The features of language that are paralinguistic are critical as they directly influence the message. Better conversation can be realized by being more aware of the subtle nuances of verbal communication by promoting deeper understanding and connection with others.

Speed or Rate of Speaking

Speaking faster or rapid rates of speech are linked to composure and self-assurance. One should try to speak at a rate similar to the individual they are communicating with. In the TV series "Young & Hungry" watch a single episode and focus on Gabi Diamond. In the TV series, Gabi Diamond speaks fast, and this makes her look like she is exhibiting composure and self-assurance.

However, if you watch several episodes, you will realize that she speaks fast to hide her insecurities and disappointments with love largely due to her quick nature of approaching love issues. Against this backdrop, speaking rapidly may suggest composure and self-assurance but it is not necessarily the true status of the individual.

Rhythm

Most languages exhibit unique rhythms and rhythm is critical especially for the English language. A person from Singapore and one from France will speak at a different speed and rhythm. In most cases, people will speak a second language at a rhythmical pace similar to their native language.

The overall aim of acknowledging rhythm is that you should try to speak at the same rhythm with the individual and the chosen rhythm should be the one that is slower than the other. At one point you tried having a conversation with a person that is not a native speaker of English and you had to slow down the conversation to enhance understanding.

To appreciate the criticality of rhythm, search YouTube for "Kids stories English India" and note the rhythm of Indian speakers of English. You will realize that the speakers try to speak close to the rhythm of their native language. Again, go to YouTube and search for "President's speech Uganda, Kenya, Nigeria or Zambia." You will observe that the speaking rhythm is close to the native language rhythm of the speaker.

As suggested, the person with a fast rhythm has to adjust to the slower rhythm. Search YouTube for "BBC interview with Uganda's president Museveni" or "CNN interview with Kenya's President Kenyatta." In many instances of these interviews, you will realize that the interview tries to slow their usual rhythm of speaking to match the relatively slow rhythm of these African countries' presidents.

On the contrary, if you voice the person with the slow rhythm to match up to your fast pace then the conversation will negatively be affected as the individual will have to rush their thoughts and reactions.

Volume

Speaking loud suggests that one is assertive, confident, and bold. Think of a politician or any leader that you recognize. Chances are that the individual speaks loud enough which shows that the person is confident and assured of what he or she is saying.

When addressing the entire school, your college principal spoke with loud volume which indicated authority and certainty of what he or she was saying. On the other hand, speaking with low volume shows shyness and insecurity. For instance, in school, the groups that had not done adequate preparation during the presentation probably spoke with low volume.

The ones that had researched and fine-tuned their work spoke confidently. If you are a parent, you will notice that if your child has done something awkward then he or she will reply in a low, almost muffled voice.

Pitch

Speaking with a high-pitched voice makes one sound childlike. Lower pitches are largely associated with higher credibility, authority, and maturity. Try listening to Bernadette Rostenkowski, the character wife to Howard Wolowitz in the TV series "The Big Bang Theory." She features from season 6 onwards. Take note of Bernadette Rostenkowski's pitch in the TV series.

The most important thing is that the pitch you choose should be your most powerful vocal range. You should not force a lower-pitched voice even if it is considered more credible as you risk losing the vocal power. For emphasis, speaking in a low-pitched voice indicates that you have owned the space and are confident in what you are expressing.

Most people find people with deep voices as appealing to listen to and hold a conversation with. Men have an advantage when it comes to low-pitch voices and this easily makes them come across as composed and in charge. The low pitch voice is a critical element of talk therapy as it gives reassurance and calming effect to the target person.

Inflection

Vocal variety or inflection concerns the variations in the pitch of the voice. Some contexts demand variations in pitch such as when narrating a story to children while other contexts demand less variation in pitch such as in the corporate world. A few singing exercises when showering can help improve tone variation of the voice. The other great way to practice is to record and listen to oneself to analyze the quality of your inflection.

When listening to someone, pay attention to inflection. A person that shows expected tonal variation of the voice is speaking naturally and probably is truthful. People that speak a monotone are likely disinterested or not being truthful. However, some instances may justify speaking with no tonal variation in casual contexts.

For instance, people that are not native speakers of English are likely to speak with a flat tone and this because they lack the native perception of the choice of the words used.

Additionally, most people when reading a text are likely to use a flat tone as opposed to speaking their minds literally. Equally important, some cultures and languages favor variation of tone. For instance, American English and Lingala language are widely spoken in the Democratic Republic of Congo naturally demands tonal variation of the voice.

The phonetics of these languages give the speakers the quality of varying tone compared to say the Swahili language widely spoken in East Africa. In this manner, the cultural context of the language may enhance or lower the degree of inflection when one is speaking.

Lastly, a tonal variation of the voice does not imply shouting as one can speak softly but vary the tone.

Quality

The attribute of voice that enables you to distinguish one voice from another is known as the quality of the voice. For instance, identifying a voice as feminine or aloof constitutes the quality of the voice. The quality of a voice is a function of pitch, rate, and volume of voice. Even though the quality of voice can be learned, in most cases it is innate. Some people are born with a commanding voice or feminine voice. The quality of voice is largely monetized when one decides to work as a musician, narrator or news anchor. Despite having different voice qualities, some contexts seek and use different voice qualities especially in animation movies and general movies where the different quality of voices are critical to eliciting laughter and relatable aspects of the production.

Perhaps the best illustration of different voice qualities is the TV animation series, "Family Guy." Search for an episode of "Family Guy" and notice the different voice qualities. Before you search, kindly appreciate that some of the content may sound offensive to people with disabilities, and ethnic minorities. However, most of the content is standard with a touch of humor. Listen to the quality of voice of the character Louis and that of the character Peter Griffin. Again, listen to the quality of the voice of Joe and that of Stewie, all characters. You can also look for any animation and I suggest "The Storks" and "Penguins of Madagascar" to appreciate the quality of voice. Most animation movies present different voice qualities within a short period of time enabling you to register and analyze them.

Tone

With respect to voice, tone regards the intensity of the voice. The tone of a voice reveals more about the emotions behind the words being spoken. If the listener is assertive then he or she will quickly connect and create a rapport with someone on the telephone by utilizing aspects of paralinguistic communication. Creating a rapport can be enhanced through matching and mirroring vocal attributes devoid of mockery. All these lead to greater understanding and more effective paralinguistic communication. Realizing awareness of your paralinguistic vocal strengths will enable one to subtly influence the speaking and listening so that one comes across as a powerful communicator.

Equally important is that the loudness of a voice varies across cultures. For instance, men in Saudi Arabia may sound aggressive when compared against the loudness of voice in the United States. Among Arabs, a soft tone implies weakness. Personal social class also impacts the loudness of voice with people in lower classes using lower volumes when speaking. The tone of the voice is what feels that someone is angry.

For non-Americans outside America, they may struggle to notice the sarcasm in the laughter of some Americans. Americans tend to apply sarcasm in speech and laughter that non-Americans may miss unless they understand tone. When speaking or interacting with a non-American one should understand that the person may not get the sarcasm, and this may impede effective conversation. Overall, when using tonal variation to elicit sarcasm, one should be careful with respect to the ethnic and nationality composition of the audience.

BODY LANGUAGE AT A BUSINESS MEETING OR MAKING A PRESENTATION

Business meetings may involve people you already work with or people you've just met whom you might need to sign a deal with. If the meeting is with people, you're meeting for the first time and have to impress, most of the body language for a job interview would also apply. Here are more tips that will also work when dealing with co-workers.

It's important to try to gauge how the person you're talking to is feeling. Take a look at the individual's eyes. If they're downcast, and the person is seemingly avoiding you, then something has to be worked out. Other signs of defensiveness, conflict in points of view or unwillingness to cooperate are arms folded across chest, the whole body facing away from you, feet facing away or towards the exit, and absence of open gestures. Watch also for pursed or tight lips and arms tightly grasped. Frequent blinking and eyes darting from side to side also signify boredom and a desire to find a way out. Your sensitivity to these signals will help you respond in a way that will help ease the tension and make the others more receptive and agreeable.

Be prepared

These are things that you can do before facing everyone else, to prep you to make a good impression. You must have all the data or all the information you'll need to persuade, convince, present or defend, or whatever the purpose of the meeting will be. Not knowing the facts or the background about what you have to discuss will leave you groping or bluffing, and this will come out in your body language.

Stand tall with your feet apart, exposing your neck, chest and stomach areas. Put your hands on your hips to appear bigger than you are. This is a power pose. Even if you don't feel powerful or confident, assuming such a pose sends a message to your brain to release more testosterone that will make you truly confident.

Listen

Whether you're the boss or subordinate, it always helps to use body language that shows that you are listening and that you value what the other person is saying. This requires eye contact, nodding, as well as open arm and leg movements. Touch a closed hand to your chin or cheek, with your index finger pointing towards your forehead to show that you are digesting and evaluating what you hear. Resting your head on your hand will indicate boredom, however. Simply tilting your head, a bit to the side will signal to the speaker that you are listening and interested.

Use a pen or pointer

A big chunk of the information people process comes from what they see. Using a pen or pointer to direct the listener's gaze to the information you are describing reinforces his perception of it. After introducing the information visually as well as verbally, subtly bringing the pointer or pen to the level of your eyes will bring the listener's gaze you yours, making a powerful impact and ensuring that the information is clearly embedded in the listener's mind.Using open palm gestures while doing this and explaining will make this a positive experience for the listener.

Nod

Nodding encourages a person to trust and to open up because it signals your agreement, understanding and non-aggression. If you nod to show agreement, the other person relaxes, loses any aggression he may harbor and begins to trust in you. As your nod your head, the listener will unconsciously find himself nodding as well and becoming more open to your ideas.

Show your openness

Use open palms, tilted head, eye contact, smiling and legs pointed toward the person to signal "I am with you." This will make the person more willing to work with you.

Do some mirroring

People who are close to each other, like married couples, begin to resemble each other because of mirroring, this is the tendency to copy or imitate a person's body language.

This is normally subconscious and is part of our programming to survive. This was said to have started in the womb where the fetus learned to match the rhythms of its mother's womb. It may also be a primitive survival tactic, when being different or not belonging could have cost an individual his life.

Although this occurs naturally when people spend time together and share common goals or beliefs, a little conscious mirroring can send signals to the other person that you have similar goals and that you support each other.

Enlarge your space

Open up and expose your neck, chest, and stomach. Stand straight and tall, with your arms on your hips to appear bigger. You will be perceived as confident and authoritative, and you will feel bolder as well.

Smile

The human brain has been wired in such a way that people automatically respond to a smile. A sincere smile can automatically diffuse tension and resistance. Using humor will automatically break barriers in communication.

Use a convincing voice

People are convinced more by their impression of you than by the facts you may be presenting them with. A deep and smooth voice is said to be pleasant and more convincing to the listener. It means that one must be reasonably relaxed and composed to produce this kind of voice. Humming can help warm up your voice before speaking.

Take a good look

Some people are not so good at picking up subtle signs, so you have to make more assertive signals. If you're the boss or a person who's supposed to be in charge, there will be times when you'll have to take an extra step to make this felt. Imagine that a person has a "third eye" on his forehead just slightly above and between the eyebrows, sort of like a Cyclops. Turn your gaze on that third eye and don't go down. This is a power gaze that works well on particularly belligerent subordinates. Narrowing your eyelids and not blinking will make this look more intimidating.

Signal that the conversation is over

You can do the same or turn your body slightly away from the other person to signal that you have to get back to work. This usually works although you may have to say outright that you have to get back to work if the other person hasn't picked up on your signals.

Make a power exit

It's not over until you're outside of the door. Be aware that people will be looking at your back as you leave, so make sure it will give the right impression. There shouldn't be any thread hanging from the hemline of your clothing and your shoes should be shined at the back. Look back just before you step out, smile and close the door behind you. People's last memory of you before you step out should be of you smiling.

Six Body Language Mistakes

Try not to worry if you've seen yourself making some of these mistakes, we all do it! Looking at mistakes is one of the best ways of learning as stopping yourself from doing something is generally easier than remembering to add in a small gesture to your interactions every time, you're speaking to someone.

The Boy Who Cried Wolf

One of the most important things to do with body language is to be consistent in what you are saying with your body and what you are thinking in your mind.

You can only lie to a certain degree before your body starts betraying you, and whether or not you are trying to deceive someone, they may begin to think this is the case if you are portraying too much confidence when the situation doesn't warrant it.

Why You Gotta Be So Rude?

There's not much point in learning about body language if you are simply going to ignore what you have learnt. If you're listening to a talk you find boring don't stare at the clock, continuously glance at your watch, sit so low in your chair that you might fall out, or start fidgeting. This is instead a great time to practice observing body language!

If someone talks to you, then make sure to provide eye contact and use body language that conveys interest and attentiveness. This is unless you would rather not convey interest towards them, then do the opposite. It can be difficult to give someone attention and respect with your body language if you feel nervous, if you don't like them, or if you are tired and simply not interested in what they are saying. The best option here is to just sit or stand up straight and try to make as much eye contact as possible until an opportunity to exit the interaction arises.

—

If you find that you do get nervous or socially awkward try to manage your environment to assist you. Sitting sideways from someone can make things less intense and confrontational as it creates more open space and proximity between others, as can writing things down to give you a break from looking at others.

Being Slightly Too Pedantic

So, you've learnt which aspects of your body language convey happiness and respect? Don't start trying to use them like magic spells in a video game. Body language needs to be used naturally or else others will think you are hiding something, or you are just irritatingly happy or good-willed. If you are trying to sell something or intimidate people with your body language don't be surprised if they notice what you are doing. Hand gestures should be used sparingly and should not risk be hitting other people in the face. Your posture doesn't always have to be perfect so that you look like a soldier on parade. The main aim with body language should be to trick yourself into having a particular emotion, not into tricking others that you feel that way as the former works better with the latter having the opposite effect of what you are intending to achieve.

Lacking Assertiveness

Assertive might not be the correct word here, but it lets you know how you need to behave more than the vague idea of 'not being confident'. What you need to avoid is defaulting to being too submissive when you are questioned or when speaking to someone that you need to connect with. This can mean making sure you maintain eye contact and only breaking it by looking to the side and not glancing down. It can mean being willing to question others when you think something isn't right and directing the topic of a conversation.

In more general terms you will want to avoid childish or wild hand gestures. If you find you are waving your hands around too much, then gently place them in your lap or on your table. You don't want to seem flakey or out of control by being too expressive with your body language. Having a limp handshake is perhaps the most infamous example of a lack of assertion.

World Dominance

Yes, life isn't fair. On the one hand you can seem too weak and feeble and then, on the other hand, sometimes people will find you too domineering. This is why reading body language is just as important as using it correctly. Many believe that showy displays of confidence and bravado are the best option in most scenarios. But confidence comes in many forms, and in certain situations, trying to show off or being too intense will make it seem like you are trying too hard to impress others, or that you simply lack self-awareness.

If you are dealing with someone that is more reserved, quiet, nervous, or perhaps not very confident in themselves, you should adapt to that. These people will generally want space and lower-energy body language from you. This means not getting too close, not putting pressure on them to speak up, and not being open with your body to the point of putting them on edge. Reading this can be difficult at first, and you will need to learn how to match energy levels with other people. Mirroring and matching and reading other people through baselines will help you a lot in this regard.

Knowing your place in a social hierarchy is important as well. If you try to be too assertive towards someone that is your superior, or even just an elder, this can lead them into thinking you are disrespectful and arrogant. This might not always be as obvious as it first appears either. You might technically outrank the office secretary, but if they have been with the business a long time you will want to show them respect as they may have more power than you in certain matters despite the fact you 'outrank' them in the office hierarchy.

Insensitivity

Following on from the last mistake, being insensitive to the feelings and norms of the place you are in is often a big mistake when it comes to body language. In most cases if you're being insensitive with your body language, it's because you aren't being sensitive with your thoughts and communication. However, sometimes you might have your arms crossed across your chest because you are cold, or you find it comfortable. So, make sure you pay attention to what you are doing when it matters most. There is a learning curve in certain situations, and it can be steep. If you've never had to care for an injured person before it is difficult to make sure you are using the right kind of comforting body language.

People who haven't been around children will find the body language to use for them can be very bewildering at times because it doesn't match what they've been used to for a long time as children aren't generally accustomed to social norms. Make sure to be alert, aware, and sensitive to the situation you find yourself in, what a person might expect from you and what you are doing with your body and whether it meets their expectations.

How to Have a Positive Effect on Others

Part of coming across as respectable to other people and getting along with them is projecting confidence and positivity. Someone who is seen as a positive person will have a much easier time connecting to a wider range of people and will also get to enjoy better opportunities in life, due to their approachable nature. This makes it highly important to learn how to come across this way. It's not as hard as it seems to become a positive influence for those around you, and you can start right now. Here are some simple actions that can have a positive effect on others:

Approachable Facial Expressions

A genuine smile tells the other person you are warm, confident and approachable. This build trusts.

Subtle Mirroring

Match the other person's movements in a subtle way. This helps build rapport through establishing a common ground. It also shows your similarities as you mimic others.

People will naturally observe this even if they aren't aware of it on the surface and will instantly like you more.

Nodding

Nodding while someone is talking shows you are engaged and listening. So many people are used to people being distracted while they are talking, so this is a simple way to show you care and are truly hearing the other person and listening.

Also, you can nod while you are talking to help influence the person to agree with you. It is no guarantee, but when you nod while asking a question, people often unknowingly nod as well, signifying they are agreeing with what you are saying.

Don't Sit Down

Standing up helps you feel powerful and confident. This is useful when giving presentations. Just make sure not to stand over anyone, as that is a sign of a threat to most people.

Be Mindful of your Head Position

Tilting your head or body toward someone shows you are interested. If you make others feel important then you have the opportunity to positively influence them.

Pointing your Feet

The way your feet point says a lot about whether you want to be where you are or not. Much like head positioning, the position of your feet can also have a subconscious effect on someone. Pointing your feet towards someone shows you are interested. It is a positive signal that builds trust. Pointing your feet away, on the other hand, shows that you subconsciously are waiting for a chance to escape as soon as possible.

WHAT CAN MASTERING BODY LANGUAGE DO FOR YOU?

It's possible to improve your life and interpersonal interactions greatly by becoming mindful of your nonverbal cues. Research shows that having correct nonverbal language will aid you in the following ways:

Less Misunderstandings

This can help with connection with others, meaning that you are less likely to be misunderstood. Since misunderstandings are at the base of most negative interactions and resentment, this is a must.

Better Performance

The right posture will help you with your performance, since it directly impacts how you come across and the mood, you're in. Utilizing "power postures" will help you feel more confident. You can also embody the idea of determination in your posture to make yourself feel stronger and more confident. Small shifts in your nonverbal cues can have a great effect on your existence, overall. Here are some specific ways that this can happen for you.

A Posture of Power

Our body language has a direct role in the people we are, whether we're aware of it or not. This simple factor directly shapes our personalities, abilities, power, and confidence levels. Not only does the way you carry yourself send others a clear message about you, but it sends your brain a clear message, as well, and impacts the way you act and feel.

Our animal relatives show their dominance and power by making themselves larger, expanding, taking up more room, and stretching their bodies out. In other words, establishing power is all about opening your body up, and people do this as well.

If you are feeling nervous, small, or incapable, simply open your body up and pay attention to the

---

way your mood shifts. You should feel suddenly much more capable and self-assured.

You might, for example, wish you feel more confident or powerful in situations where you are interviewing for a job and wish to showcase your abilities and assertiveness. You might also wish to show that you're confident in a classroom situation or a leadership position. As you walk into a negotiation, you would definitely want to send a message that you know what you want and are well-aware of your own abilities.

For situations like this, or any others you need a confidence boost in, you can stand erect, with your shoulders pushed back, your stance wide, and your head upward. Raise up your arms to make a "Y" as in the YMCA dance, and you will instantly feel more powerful and energetic. What is it about this posture that helps us feel better and more confident? It affects our hormones, resulting in a couple of key ingredients in the feeling of dominance. These are cortisol (the hormone of stress) and testosterone (the hormone of dominance). Males who are in high, alpha positions of power in groups of primates have low levels of cortisol and high levels of testosterone, but this isn't just primates. Effective and powerful people in leadership positions have the same pattern, meaning that they are assertive and powerful, but don't react strongly to stress.

Even in tough situations, they are able to stay calm and handle business effectively. Research shows that adopting the power position we just told you about for a minimum of a couple minutes will lower your levels of cortisol while boosting testosterone. In other words, you will be priming your brain to deal with whatever situations might pop up during the day.

MORE POSTURES FOR IMPROVING YOUR LEVELS OF PERFORMANCE

The posture of our body directly influences our mind, which results in our specific behaviors and actions. This means that if we can convince our physical bodies to lead our minds to more positive places, our performance will skyrocket as a result. Here are some postures that are recommended by professionals for positive results.

- Tensing up for Willpower: If you're in a situation that calls for more willpower, you should tense your muscles up. This posture shows your body that you're tensed and ready for anything, no matter what. This will send the message to your brain that resilience is needed on a mental level.

- Hand Gestures for Persuasion: If you're in a position where you need to persuade other people in conversation, make sure you utilize gestures of the hands. This shows that you believe in what you're saying and also helps you come across as more convincing. Others will feel more positive about you if you do this.

- Cross your Arms for Persistence: Having crossed arms can mean that you're closed off, which is bad in certain circumstances. In others, however, this is a useful frame of mind. You might, for example, be in a situation where stubbornness is a good quality and you need it to stay persistent. This is a good time to cross your arms.

How to gain the Advantage in Body Language:

Body language is a whole new world that can change your life. When it comes to any situation that handles interactions with others, it's a must for being successful. Here are some tips for getting ahead in this area.

- Raising the Eyebrows: When someone is out in public and sees someone they know, their eyebrows will move up automatically, just a tiny bit. No matter what culture, this response is present. The good news here is that you can start using this to your own benefit any time you meet a new person. Try to do it in the first few seconds that you're talking to them. Raising your eyebrows just a little bit will make you appear more approachable and friendly, creating a positive connection between you and the other person.

- Remember Times you were Enthusiastic: Having charisma just means that you have enthusiasm and that it shows clearly to other people. This means that wanting to look charismatic to others requires simply appearing enthusiastic. In order to do this at will, simply call to your mind another time that made you feel enthusiastic. Once you re recalling this past event that made you very excited and enthusiastic, this will come across in your nonverbal cues, showing that you're charismatic and confident. This is a contagious effect and others will feel more positive from noticing your enthusiasm and charisma.

- Smile for more Resilience: If you're faced with a hard task, you can make it feel easier to yourself by smiling. The body's natural reaction to reaching exhaustion is making a pained grimace. However, experiments have shown that smiling increases your ability to press on and keep going through that feeling. Athletes were shown to be able to do a few more reps if they started smiling during their performance.

Making a grimace sends your brain the message that you aren't able to continue doing what you're doing. Your brain then reacts to that by pumping you feel of stress chemicals, adding to your exhaustion and difficulty. Smiling, on the other hand, shows your brain that you are able to keep going, resulting in a better performance and more resilience.

Using these cues will help you a lot with your general positivity and how others perceive it. Shifting your nonverbal cues and body language will influence the way you're perceived by those around you, as well as how you see yourself. On top of this, your facial expressions and postures are always sending your brain messages which then influence the hormones your body is releasing. This is a great power to have if you're aware of it and use it in the right way, but not being aware of it can have negative results and effects, not only on yourself, but on others. Take the power into your own hands and become more positive by using this connection.

The Secret Is in The Breath

There are various ways you can read a person's body language. You can read it by their arm and leg movements, facial expressions, smiles, or eye contact. But did you know that the way you breathe has meanings also?

Emotions and the way you breathe have connections. You can read a person's feeling by watching their breathing. If your emotions change, the way you breathe can be affected. See if you can notice breathing patterns in your coworkers, family, friend, or partner. They might not tell you exactly how the person is feeling, and it could depend on a specific situation.

- Sighing might be a signal of sadness, hopelessness, or relief

When you sigh, you let out a deep, long breath that has an audible sound. Someone might sigh if they feel relieved like after a struggle has passed. They are probably thankful that this struggle is over. A sigh could also show hopelessness or sadness, like someone waiting for their date to show up. It might also show disappointment and tiredness.

- Rapid, heavy breathing might show fear and tiredness

You might have just seen a person rob a place and they are being chased by the police. You notice they are both breathing very rapidly. This is because the lungs need more oxygen because they are exerting a lot of energy due to the running. Their bodies are feeling tired, and their lungs are trying to keep up. We will feel the same effects when we get scared. This happens because when we experience fear, our lungs need extra oxygen, so we start to breathe faster. You can easily see when someone has been scared or running by noticing how they are breathing.

- Deep breathing could indicate attraction, love, excitement, fear or anger

Breathing deeply is the easiest breathing patterns to spot. If someone suddenly begins to hold their breath, they might be feeling a bit scared. If a person takes a deep breath and then shouts, they might be angry.

People, who feel excited, are surprised, or experience shock could suck in a deep breath. They can also take in a deep breath and hold it for a second or so. If their eyes begin to glow, this could indicate they are excited or surprised.

A person might begin to breathe deeply if they are attracted to someone. You might notice someone take a deep breath in, suck in their stomach, and push out their chest in order to impress someone they are attracted to.

Body Language Applications

Body language and self-esteem go hand in hand. This allows for a wonderful mechanism to observe and monitor how people behave and feel. Awareness of our body language is essential for becoming effective and persuasive communicators. Hence, there are several applications for using, reading, and changing body language.

Therapeutic Applications

Body language plays a major role in counseling, NLP, and hypnotherapy. For psychologists, body language not only allows them a way to read their clients' emotional state, but also gives them a way to build rapport. Observing the client's body language can help the psychologist to read how the client responds to a certain discussion or line of questioning.

Body language speaks when we can't. Health care professionals have known this for some time. A great many studies have been conducted in it, and psychology academic studies for professionals including modalities on body language. Common issues which can be examined and treated through the use of body language include:

Bi polarity

Individuals with this condition suffer a chemical imbalance that leads to severe depression and the inability to make decisions. They often have a low self-esteem that accompanies this disorder, and it is incredibly difficult to understand effectively or treat correctly. Using body language, the person with bipolarity can be taught to manage their daily situations, and considering the link between body language and emotion, they can also enjoy relief by being trained to use positive body language.

This is a way for them to use their own body language to persuade their emotions to stabilize and improve. For their families, body language reading is also an effective way to monitor their loved one's state and intervene before incidents happen. Depression can often go unnoticed, and people will rarely speak out about it. They are not likely to say: "I'm feeling depressed."

Low self-esteem

Many of us have suffered the devastating effects of low self-esteem in one way or another. The first victim is our ability to progress in life. A positive belief in yourself is needed if you are to convince the rest of the world to believe in you. People can be trained in positive body language such as the open position, making eye contact, lifting the head. It's a case of faking it until you feel it. With enough repetitive use of persuasive body language, you can even convince yourself that you are stronger than you believe.

Trauma

Survivors of trauma suffer from a loss of power, feelings of inadequacy, and loss of confidence. They also have the burden of guilt where they hold themselves responsible for what happened to them. Whether the trauma is due to a violent act such as an assault or rape, a natural disaster or loss in their family, the emotional state of these individuals is reflected in their body language or the change thereof. Where body language may have been positive and inviting before the incident, the person may now display negative body language, such as crossed arms, slumping, excessive facial touching, and nervous ticks such as repetitive movement. With effective counseling, their progress to recovery can be tracked through counseling and monitoring their body language.

Abuse

Abuse can be physical, emotional, and sexual in nature, but whichever of these it is, there is bound to be an overwhelming sense of a loss of power. The victim may need to be convinced that they can regain their power and that it is okay to trust people. Body language is extremely efficient in this regard. Helping these survivors of abuse establish strong body language will increase their sense of their own strength. Suffering abuse at the hands of another human being is also linked to a loss of trust in people and the world around them. By helping the abuse victim to understand the body language of others, they can be aided in evaluating the world and those around them in terms of what they see, not what they fear. This is in itself already great empowerment to the abuse victim, as they can become a participant in life again, and feel like they have the power to make informed decisions.

Self-development

Being an effective communicator is one of life's great skills that will open doors and lead to the emboldening of the self. Self-development programs often include modalities on body language where the participants are trained in the uses of positive body language and assertiveness.

Group dynamics

People can be classed as two groups: introverts and extroverts. Introverts, as we know, are those people who tend to thrive in one-on-one communications and prefer to spend more time alone; while extroverts are the life of the party and go through life with a the-more-the-merrier attitude. Introverts often suffer a form of depression based on social settings. They do not do well in groups. As a result, their communication within a group dynamic tends to fizzle. Yet, communication is a learned skill. Like we learn the words, sentence structures, and grammar of a new language, we can also learn the way in which body language works.

Depression

People suffering from depression tend to convince themselves that they are not worthy, that they are to blame for some usually imaginary flaw, and that they are being judged by everyone around them. In the worst cases, this can lead to extreme paranoia. People with depression sometimes think that everyone else has it good, while they alone are suffering. In creating awareness of body language, they can begin to see the world in a more realistic sense and realize that people everywhere go through trying times and that they are not alone.

By learning to focus on using positive body language they can also begin to manage their condition, as this will encourage feelings of well-being.

OCD

This condition is known for the repetitive behavior that someone engages in to make themselves feel in control of their lives. At the root of this tragic condition lies the fear of a loss of power and a profound distrust in themselves and in others. In extreme cases, this can even extend to excessive washing of hands to remove imaginary germs and then avoiding people because people have germs.

People with OCD tend to have a very negative view of the world, and their only safety comes from their repetitive behaviors. Using body language, they can be trained to notice positive feelings in others and to begin incorporating that into themselves. As they learn to project a positive self-image, they will feel their stress levels diminish, which will lead to a reduction of their anxiety-driven obsessions. When they feel more balanced, they will begin to develop trust in themselves and those around them.

Destructive body imagery (bulimia and obesity)

Poor body image is a tragic and very destructive condition to suffer from. It goes with low self-esteem, lack of trust, feelings of abandonment, and severe depression. Bulimia leads the sufferer to obsessively lose weight, while obesity is a condition where the sufferer wants to fill themselves due to their own emotional disabilities.

Both these conditions are associated with a loss of reality. These people begin to see the world not as it is, but as they believe it to be, and their world view is almost always negative. They eat, or refuse to eat, to hide from the world and themselves.

Body language is a way to find a connection back to the real world. In reading the body language being projected by those around us, we can begin to see that there are loads of people who are just like us. We are not alone. Using positive body language is one of the therapeutic ways to recover a sense of self that is realistic and beneficial.

THE BIOLOGICAL FEEDBACK MECHANISM OF BODY LANGUAGE

Due to our loss of trust in other humans, we often turn to animals for comfort and assurance. We read into what people do, what they say, how they say it, and how they react to us. A salesman will do this on a second-by-second basis where they monitor the body language of the client and adjust their body language to match. Techniques such as mirroring, open position, advancing or retreating, and touching can be used to have an effect on the other person, and monitor how persuasive we are being on them. If they have begun to trust us enough, they will begin to do something we want; in which case, we will trust them since they've done something for us. This endless, nonverbal loop is known as a biological feedback mechanism.

TRAINING AND EXERCISES

There are numerous academies and colleges that strive to train people in body language detection and application. They mention facts and case-studies, what to do and what not to do; however, not many of them detail exactly how to improve your body language in a step-by-step way. When considering the activities and desired results, we suggest the following steps be followed:

Look

Look at the world around you. Notice the people in it and how they interact with each other. Identify people in similar situations to those that challenge you. This could be someone applying for a promotion at work, asking a girl on a date, and even haggling for a discount. Each situation will use the same skills but in different ways. It all boils down to body language.

Take notes if you like or snapshot the interactions. This may seem like stalking behavior to some, but it is called vicarious learning in psychological circles. You learn from the behavior, whether successful or not, of others.

Practice

This will require some bravery, which is perhaps why people do crazy things in foreign lands where no one knows them. Find some friends or set up a hidden camera if you have to or go to obedience training with your dog. The goal is to place yourself in a situation where you can practice some of the skills and how they can be used.

If you feel overwhelmed, you can practice at home with a mirror. You might even find some online help with an online counselor who can perhaps observe you over Skype.

Evaluate

Look at the recording you made of yourself or talk to friends who are helping you. Don't look at your awkwardness; rather, focus on each body language technique, how you applied it, and what the response to it was. You may even give yourself a score or write down what you need to focus on. Remember to celebrate the successes, no matter how small. Then it's time to repeat step two, practice. It may seem like an incredibly arduous task to learn body language, but it certainly is worth it. These skills of using space, posture, facial expressions, eye contact, gesture, and touch are vital to leading a fulfilling life that has less conflict and misunderstanding in it.

CONCLUSION

In everyday life, human onlookers are incredibly capable in perceiving faces, separating among them, and utilizing them to infer a huge scope of data, be it about static highlights like age, sex or character, or variable highlights like look bearing, lip developments or enthusiastic states. Typically, during the free review of entire faces, spectators will concentrate their look on explicit parts, with an articulated inclination to concentrate on the eye locale when attempting to recognize distinctive passionate demeanors. In any case, there is in like manner solid proof that every fundamental articulation of feeling is related to a particular arrangement of highlights, for instance, with the eyes significant for dread acknowledgment or the mouth for recognizing bliss.

Besides, if spectators can decipher this data in an effective manner, they should utilize every one of these analytic highlights to various degrees, contingent upon the feeling being referred to. In studies where appearances are halfway veiled, and onlookers can just utilize constrained data in every preliminary, a normal face can be remade, reflecting which regions are most firmly connected with a right reaction. Every feeling articulation would thus be able to be depicted by an alternate arrangement of analytic regions, conceivably permitting to separate every articulation similarly well from all others.

However, arrangements of indicative regions may likewise mirror a trademark example of similitude between certain feelings, clarifying specific sorts of efficient disarrays among articulations and permitting to more readily see how the various articulations are spoken to in the onlooker's psyche. Charles Darwin in his initial research on the articulation of feelings previously proposed that contradicting feelings like indignation and dread (for example battle or flight) will be communicated by the body and face in a contradictory manner, and numerous mental models attempted to delineate similitude or restriction of feelings in regard to their event and abstract understanding.

Exact help for certain parts of these models originates from concentrates on the acknowledgment of articulations, where, for instance, satisfaction is perceived the best and befuddled the least in accordance with the way that it is the main positive of the fundamental feelings and subsequently ought to be generally particular. Likewise, various reports of orderly missteps or disarrays between articulations exhibit that outrage and appall, just as dread and shock are most often befuddled.

These feelings are additionally conceptualized as comparative, they would say. Concerning way they are communicated in the face, effectively befuddled looks can be portrayed by a mostly covering set of activity units, with brought down eyebrows in displeasure and disturb or the cocked eyebrows and eye tops in dread and shock, together with showing a closeness of experience, demeanor, and physical appearance. In the

122

present investigation, we, in this way, solicited whether acknowledgment from outward appearances depends on a one-of-a-kind arrangement of highlights for every feeling, and got these highlights from the eyewitnesses' acknowledgment execution. Spectators were given covered faces which were successively uncovered part-by-part and must be perceived as quick as could reasonably be expected.

Regions of the face whose exposure regularly prompted quick and exact reactions were recognized for every demeanor, permitting to, in this way, think about the appearances and develop an illustrative space in which countenances are gathered by how also they are seen. This plans to supplement past investigations with covered faces by not just reproducing the visual information that offers ascend to address acknowledgment, yet additionally determining a numerical measurement for every territory of the face and consolidate these territories into examples that have the most elevated indicative worth.